Moses
AND THE Long Walk

The story of the journey
to the Promised Land
Exodus 16–17, 32 for children

Written by Joanne Bader
Illustrated by Johanna van der Sterre

Now Moses was a special man,
For he was picked by God
To lead His people, Israel,
Onto the promised sod.

The Promised Land, Canaan by name,
Was very far away.
God showed the way with fire at night
And with a cloud by day.

They lived in tents along the way.
They left their homes behind
In Egypt where they'd worked
 as slaves
 For masters so unkind.

It was a very long, long trip
 Across the barren lands.
 The people oftentimes forgot
 That they were in God's hands.

The people griped and fussed and crabbed
At Moses, and they said,
"Why'd you lead us out of Egypt
'Cause now we'll soon be dead!

"We have no food that we can eat,
And not a drop to drink!"
But Moses told them, "God will help
No matter what you think."

At night God sent some quail as food,
Which was their meat to eat.
And in the morning bread appeared
To make their meal complete.

God gave them water when they asked.
It came in special ways.
Once, when Moses struck a rock,
The water poured out for days.

Their enemies sometimes attacked
And then there was a fight.
But God told Moses, "I will help
So they will know My might!"

It was here in the wilderness
God gave His Ten Commands
To Moses high up on a hill
Above the desert lands.

While Moses was up on the mount,
The people got so bold.
They made a calf and worshiped it—
An idol made of gold.

They sinned against the Lord their God,
And Moses told them so,
"You must repent for what you've done."
And they were full of woe.

Then Moses talked to God in prayer;
"Forgive them," was his plea.
And God forgave
  His people then
As He does you and me.

It took them 40 years in all
To reach the Promised Land.
The Lord stayed with them
  all the way
And blessed them with His hand.

They were the children that He loved,
Just as He loves us, too.
He guided and protected them,
Just as He cares for you.

God led His people to a place
Where He knew they'd be free.
He'll lead us to our home in heav'n—
Salvation! Victory!

Dear Parents,

This amazing story from the book of Exodus is a powerful example of God's love and faithfulness to the children of Israel and to us, His children today.

Israel whined and complained, worshiped idols, disobeyed God's commands, and even lost faith in God during their long journey to freedom. Yet God watched over them, guided them, provided for them, and protected them every step of the way. He forgave them when their trust in Him failed.

Even as we daily sin and fall short of God's expectations, He still watches over us, leads and guides us, protects and forgives us—just as He did the children of Israel. And just as He promised to deliver them from slavery in Egypt and lead them into the Promised Land, He promises to lead us from the slavery of sin to the freedom of salvation through our Savior Jesus Christ.

Remind your children that although we whine and complain, no matter how many times we need forgiveness, we have the assurance that God will always love us and forgive us, He will never leave us and He will lead us to our Promised Land—our home in heaven!

The Author